| DATE DUE | | | |
|---|---|---|---|
| | | | |
| | | | |
| | | | |
| | | | |
| | | | |
| | | | |
| | | | |
| | | | |
| | | | |
| | | | |
| | | | |
| | | | |
| | | | |

# TELEVISION
# IN
# AMERICAN
# SOCIETY

# TELEVISION IN AMERICAN SOCIETY

## BY GLENN ALAN CHENEY

A GROLIER COMPANY

FRANKLIN WATTS
NEW YORK I TORONTO I LONDON I SYDNEY I 1983
AN IMPACT BOOK

# DEDICATED TO
# YOU WHO WOULD
# RATHER READ

Library of Congress Cataloging in Publication Data
Cheney, Glenn Alan.
Television in American society.

(An Impact book)
Bibliography: p.
Includes index.
Summary: In examining America's enthrallment with television,
such aspects of the "ultimate mass medium" are explored as
television and children, television and truth, television as
business, and the future of television in the United States.
1. Television broadcasting—Social aspects—United
States—Juvenile literature. [1. Television]   I. Title.
PN1992.6.C523 1983        302.2′345′0973        83-6603
ISBN 0-531-04402-5

# CONTENTS

# TELEVISION IN AMERICAN SOCIETY

# 1

# THE ULTIMATE MASS MEDIUM

It started in 1456 when Johannes Gutenberg's printing press began turning out Bibles at a rate faster than that of a dozen monks. For the first time in history, books could be made available to the general public. A message could be duplicated and distributed in quantities never before possible. Printed material was the first mass medium, the first means of communicating with masses of people. Mass produced copies of books on philosophy, government, history, science, as well as myths, superstitions, and fiction, carried knowledge and ideas first across Europe and eventually around the globe. Worldly knowledge was now in the hands of the common people, not just in the libraries of palaces and monasteries.

When the first printing office opened in Florence, Italy, the poet Politian commented that "now the most stupid ideas can in a moment be transferred into a thousand volumes and spread abroad." And he was right. Or at least half-right. Thanks to the printing press, we have superhero comic books, trashy novels, junk mail, and pornography. But we also have newspapers, textbooks, technical manuals, and great literature. Millions of titles fill the shelves of libraries, bookstores, and newsstands. The choice of authors exceeds any reader's appetite and the variety of subjects can satisfy any need to know anything.

Five hundred years after Gutenberg, electronics supercharged the powers of mass media. First, radio enabled a message to reach millions of ears in an instant. For a brief era it was the most sophisticated means of mass communication. But now those years seem to have been only a transition stage into the age of what has been called the ultimate mass medium—television.

It reaches everywhere. Its cameras roam the world and its receiver sets are more common than refrigerators and telephones. In America, its tubes glow in 98 percent of all homes. An average American family has the television on for six and a half hours every day.

In one very important way, television is a tremendous leap forward from the print media. Watching television is a lot like really being there, separated from the action by no more than a pane of glass. Television takes its viewers across time and space to witness a vast variety of experiences that could not possibly occur in a hundred lifetimes. Viewers can see the lives of scuba divers, soldiers, cannibals, criminals, kings, farmers, and taxi drivers. They can see how the world looked a thousand years in the past or will look a thousand years in the future. Viewers have as many eyes as they have channels on their television sets.

But is this reality? Is life a series of half-hour comedies? Does a six-hour miniseries about World War II tell it like it was? Does a one-minute news report from the

White House reveal what's on the president's mind? Is Kojak a typical police officer, Laverne a typical blue-collar working woman, Mr. Rogers a typical adult, or Thundarr a typical barbarian?

No. Even in the most honest and diligent news report, let alone in fictitious entertainment, television cannot perfectly portray reality. The camera can focus only on one thing at a time, the narrator or characters can only say so much, and editors have to decide what to show and what to leave out. Consequently, television offers, at best, a series of thin slices of the real world, a version of reality created by the myriad components, from mechanical parts to people, that make up the medium of television.

But what about books, photographs, songs, plays, movies, rumors, church sermons, and stories around a campfire? These are all media. Some of them reach millions of people. Each has its peculiar frailties as a means of transmitting information, of relaying a version of reality. A book can say only so much and a word is only a symbol of the real thing. A photograph is just a small piece of the real picture and it doesn't feel, smell, sound, or move like reality. A church sermon barely begins to relate the immensity of God and humanity. And campfire stories don't even pretend to be real.

So why is television of special concern? Why do parents worry about what their children watch? Why does the government have special laws regulating the television industry? Why are psychologists and sociologists performing experiments and studies of the effects of television on adults, children, and society?

One reason is that, except for movies, television is the most realistic medium. What you see and hear on television seems a lot like what you experience in life, so it's easy to unconsciously assume that what is on television—the sex, the violence, the commercials, the cartoons—is real, true, or normal.

A second reason for the concern over television is that so many people watch it so much. There is hardly anyone who never watches. The average viewing time is over six hours, making television America's number one activity after work and sleep.

A third reason is that a given television show is a single experience that tens of millions of Americans share. On many occasions, one out of three Americans are watching exactly the same thing happen. For six hours a day, they are leading identical lives.

A fourth reason is that viewers tend to believe what television reports as fact and much of what is admitted to be fiction. They also tend to assume that because something is on television it is more important than that which is not. More Americans watch the evening news than read newspapers and they rate television news as more trustworthy than any other news medium.

A fifth, though by no means final, reason is that television programming is the product of relatively few people and corporations. America's principle source of information and entertainment is controlled almost entirely by broadcasters who want to attract an audience, and by companies that want to sell goods and services. Control by the audience is limited to changing channels or turning off the set.

For these and other reasons, television is far more than just another mass medium. It has special effects on the minds of individuals, the personalities of children, the relationships of families, the interactions within society, and the politics of the country and the world. It touches everyone's life; even if you don't watch it, you are surrounded by those who do.

What happens to people who watch television? They see handsome heroes—most often young, white males—who never make mistakes. They witness earthshaking problems that are cleared up in an hour or two. They feel the emotions involved in situations of unlikely love and conflicts of horrendous violence. Does the audience begin to think that young, white males are superior, that perfection is possible, that problems can be solved if you sit and watch them long enough, that love is quick and easy, that violence is a natural part of life, and that the good guys always win? The answer is neither no nor yes. Some people may think some of these things, but do they believe them so much that it affects their lives?

What happens to children who spend more time with television than they do with each other or with their parents, who watch television more than they play? How does this affect their imaginations, their ability to read, their curiosity, and their intelligence? How does television affect them in school, in social situations, and in adulthood?

What happens to families whose principle activity together is sitting in silence while someone else entertains them? Do they end up knowing more about Muppets than about each other? Does this affect the relationship that makes them a family rather than a group of people sharing a house? How would a family change if it had no television to bring it together?

How is a society affected if its members spend twenty-two hours a day working, sleeping, and watching television? Their jobs and dreams are different, but they all watch the same programs. How much is social normality affected by what is on television? Does video love influence social morality? Does video violence create social paranoia? Do commercials stimulate materialism? Does the common experience of sharing the shows of three networks help homogenize society, making everyone from Brooklyn to Butte somewhat the same?

How do television and politics mix? One of the greatest powers a president wields is the ability to demand television air time almost at will. Candidates for all offices spend tremendous amounts on television advertising. For $100,000, an unknown face can be broadcast from coast to coast. The same exposure can be achieved by any terrorist with a bomb and a grievance to air. But what about people with neither bombs nor money? The Constitution guarantees everyone the freedom of speech, but how many Americans get to use nation-wide television, the most powerful microphone in the world, to say what they think?

All these questions are important, but an even bigger one stands above them all: Who, if anyone, should control television? Perhaps no one should, or would that be leaving a colossal machine out of control? Perhaps the general public should regulate it, or would that make television subject to powerful special interest groups such as religious groups, professional organizations, labor unions, or organized crime? Perhaps big business should be in charge, or would that leave television serving only the interests of higher profits? Perhaps the government should hold the controls, or would that be the beginning of totalitarianism with a single political party commanding America's attention for six hours a day while it "educated" the population to serve the powers that are and always will be in control of the country? George Orwell's *1984* described such a world. It was hellish, but with the

help of government-controlled television, the people—
every one of them—learned to love it.

Neither this book nor any other has the final
answers to these questions. The best we can do is present
some evidence and discuss some possibilities. The diffi-
culty of the questions hints at the importance of their
answers. The debate in America has just begun. Praise is
as prevalent as criticism. Television is not a passing phe-
nomenon and its impact on American society may be one
of the most influential in our history.

# 2

# THE TELEVISION BUSINESS

In 1927 Philo T. Farnsworth first transmitted a televised image without the use of wire. As a test pattern, he focused his crude camera on a dollar sign. Almost sixty years later, eighty million television sets bring programs and advertisements into 98 percent of the homes in America, making the television business one of the most powerful and profitable industries in the world. The dollar sign is still behind every image that is broadcast.

An executive in the broadcast business once said that television's only reason for existence is its ability to assemble millions of people so they can see and hear an advertiser's pitch. The ultimate purpose of commercial television in America is not to entertain or educate or inform. It may in fact perform some of those services, but it does so for the same reason that any business functions—profit.

In most cases, profit comes quickly to a television station. A station broadcasting network programming on

(8)

one of the twelve principal channels can expect to make an annual profit of up to 50 percent of what it has invested and spent in operation. In two or three years it can recover its investments and be making money. Such a rate of return exceeds by far that of oil companies, car manufacturers, and virtually every other big business in the United States.

Fortunately for American viewers, the television industry can raise this money only by broadcasting what the majority of viewers want to see. Whether they want the most wholesome programs or not is a question for another chapter. But among the three commercial networks—The American Broadcasting Corporation (ABC), The Columbia Broadcasting System (CBS), and The National Broadcasting Corporation (NBC)—there is fierce competition to provide the programs that will draw the most Americans to their channel.

## NETWORKS AND AFFILIATES

Networks, the giants of the television industry, are businesses that transmit programs to television stations around the country. These stations then broadcast the programs in their local area. This is how almost everyone in America can tune in to hear Dan Rather report the news or to watch the space shuttle take off. Few of these broadcasting stations, called network affiliates, are owned or operated by a network. Each affiliate is an independent company that is paid to broadcast a network's programs in its local area.

The networks do own and operate a few stations, but the Federal Communications Commission (FCC) limits them to seven stations each, with no more than five on the popular and powerful Very High Frequency (VHF) channels that are labeled 2 through 13 on television dials. The other two must be on the weaker Ultra High Frequency (UHF) channels numbered 14 through 82. The networks have wisely chosen to own the strongest VHF stations in the largest cities. Each has a station in New York, Chicago, and Los Angeles. ABC also owns stations in Detroit and San Francisco; CBS, stations in St. Louis and Philadelphia; and NBC, stations in Washington, D.C. and Cleveland. These few stations alone reach an audience of tens of millions, giving the networks a solid foundation.

With networks transmitting programs that cost $500,000 or more per hour to produce, an expense far beyond the budgets of most individual stations, network affiliation is a most desirable relationship. Not only does the network solve a station's problem of what to broadcast during its eighteen to twenty hours on the air, but the networks will pay the station a fee for every program it clears, that is, accepts from the network and broadcasts in its local area. Affiliates usually clear about 95 percent of the network's prime-time programs, which are shown between 7:00 p.m. and 11 p.m., and about 78 percent of the off-peak programs.

Network programs come with national advertisements. The fee that an affiliate receives for clearing a program depends on the estimated number of people who watch the program and its advertisements. Affiliates receive 10 to 15 percent of the amount that advertisers pay to broadcast in that area during the cleared program. The networks also leave commercial time available for the affiliate to sell to local advertisers.

Networks willingly pay for affiliation because every additional station in the network means an addition to the total audience the network can offer to their advertisers. These national advertisers may pay the networks well over $100,000 for the opportunity to spread their commercial word across America for half a minute during prime time, when the greatest number of television sets are turned on and an average of ninety million people are watching.

Each network has 190–220 affiliates, but the numbers are always changing. An affiliate that thinks another network has more popular programming may decide to switch in order to attract more local advertisers. On the other hand, a network may drop an affiliate in a certain area so it can use a more powerful or more cooperative station. An affiliate that fails to clear enough of the network programs may suddenly find itself an independent (unaffiliated) station.

Independent stations, about 10 percent of the 753 commercial stations on the air, are in a more difficult, though not impossible, situation. They can keep 100 percent of the income generated by the local advertisements they broadcast, but they have the additional expense of buying or producing their own programs.

In-house productions by independent stations are usually low-budget shows such as local sports, news, and game and talk shows. Higher quality programs, such as films, drama, and documentaries are available from program syndicates, companies independent of networks and stations that sell video tapes of their various shows to affiliates as well as independent stations. Often, syndicate programs displace the network programming that an affiliate has rejected as not popular enough. Some of the more successful syndicate programs have been "M*A*S*H," "P.M. Magazine," "Family Feud," "All in the Family," and "The Donahue Show."

The network system of broadcasting is advantageous

to just about everyone involved. Local stations can broadcast expensive programming without major investment, networks can reach a nationwide audience without the expense and complexity of operating hundreds of stations, advertisers can display their wares in millions of homes, and television viewers can watch all they want without spending a penny in direct expenses.

## PUBLIC TELEVISION—
## AN ALTERNATIVE

To survive the competition for advertising dollars, the commercial networks must broadcast shows with wide popular appeal. Since most people usually turn on the television to see entertainment, networks cannot afford to broadcast many educational, cultural, or public affairs programs that will not attract the large audience desired by big advertisers. Therefore, such programs are most common on noncommercial stations that do not depend on advertisers for income.

Until the mid-1960s, there were 126 noncommercial television stations in the United States. Funded by colleges, school districts, local governments, and donations, most noncommercial programming was strictly educational and low-budget, often showing no more than a teacher and a blackboard—a classroom on television.

In 1967 Congress created and began funding the Corporation for Public Broadcasting (CPB). This publicly owned corporation was intended to upgrade the quality of noncommercial broadcasting and offer an alternative to commercial network programming. CPB helped organize the independent stations into a new network known as the Public Broadcasting System (PBS), which went into operation in 1969. By 1972, the number of stations in the system had increased to more than two hundred.

Until late 1982, PBS had no commercials. Its funds came from foundations, individuals, corporations, and the government, in that order. Nationwide, some 2.5 million people paid to become supporting members of 268 public television stations in 1981, tripling the number of members and dollars raised in 1973. But these sources of income were not adequate, so PBS agreed to air a very limited number of commercials between certain programs.

Since its income is not directly tied to the size of the audience, as is the case with commercial networks, PBS can better afford to sacrifice popularity and concentrate on subjects not available on other networks. "Masterpiece Theater" may never outdraw "The Muppet Show," but millions of viewers appreciate the alternative to commercial programs that are aimed at capturing the largest audience possible. It is interesting to note that a poll revealed that two-thirds of all television viewers consider public programming good or excellent while only one-third can say the same for commercial programming.

Public television has made a conscious effort to concentrate more heavily on culture and education than on certain controversial subjects. With a large portion of its budget coming from two institutions often under public criticism—government and large corporations—public television cannot afford to fall out of grace with either. This lesson has been learned through experience. In 1972, for example, President Richard Nixon vetoed a $155 million appropriation for CPB, a move many people say was caused by several PBS documentaries that harshly criticized the government. A documentary about an oil company was made less critical when that company offered a large grant to PBS. A program that blamed American banks for some of the problems of the American poor was not aired by certain PBS affiliates until banks in their areas could produce a rebuttal program.

After several such incidents, PBS toned down its public affairs programming. In cases of great controversy, it makes an effort to offer a balanced analysis rather than a direct attack. On programs like "The MacNeil/ Lehrer Report," a controversial subject is treated as a debate between opposing sides. To avoid problems, most public affairs programs focus on social ills—such as child abuse, alcoholism, inflation, unemployment—and other subjects where the concern is for solving the problem, not debating its good and bad qualities.

Today, most PBS programming is devoted to educational and cultural matters such as theater, dance, classical music performances, and documentaries on history, nature, science, and art. Children's Television Workshop, which produces "Sesame Street" and "The Electric Company," has revolutionized the concept of educational television. To reinforce adult and children's educational television there is an outreach program that offers video tapes, magazines, teacher's guides, and other materials to schools, libraries, and organizations.

The goal of PBS has been to provide something for everyone without duplicating the programming of commercial television and without becoming a channel only for the intellectually elite. Apparently it is meeting this goal. Every week, as many as 70 percent of all American televisions are tuned to PBS at least once. The audience includes people of all races and ages and all economic and educational levels. About 78 percent of the audience has less than four years of college. Almost 50 percent are blue-collar workers. About 58 percent earn less than $20,000 per year. Blacks make up about 10 percent of the audience. All these figures are roughly equal to each group's percentage of the total U.S. population. Although the total number of viewers is far lower than the total for any commercial network, this variety of viewers indicates that PBS is an important addition to American television.

# 3
# PROGRAMMING

Commercial television programming works under the same principles as democracy and capitalism. Viewers can vote for the shows they like by simply watching them, and the laws of profit and loss determine which shows will be offered to the public and which will be dropped from the marketplace. As networks strive to broadcast the programs that will attract the largest audience, advertisers calculate dollars per viewer before buying commercial time that pays for the programs and sells their clients' products.

Generally, advertisers do not care about the quality of a program as much as about the quantity of its viewers. Before investing their money in advertisements on, say, "Real People," they want to know how many people watch that show. They find this information in the ratings, which are daily, weekly, and quarterly reports on what percent of the American audience was tuned to the various channels during each half-hour time slot of the day.

The most widely accepted ratings come from the A.C. Nielsen Company, which calculates and issues reports on how many people are watching the various programs. Broadcasters live, die, and swear by the Nielsen ratings because advertisers believe in them and make their decisions based on those ratings.

Nielsen reports two types of head counts. Most important are the program ratings, which are the percentage of all television sets in America that are tuned to a certain channel at a certain time. During prime time, a program rating of 17 is satisfactory, but even a little less probably means the end of a program series. In November 1981, the top fifteen network programs had ratings ranging from 22 percent ("M*A*S*H") to 34.9 percent ("Dallas").

Nielsen also reports a program's "audience share," which is the percentage of all turned-on television sets that are tuned to each program. Networks aim for an audience share of 33 percent, are delighted with a share over 35 percent, and will probably kill a prime-time program that drops to 25 percent. Since these two rating reports predict how many people are watching each show, advertising rates are closely tied to ratings. According to one network executive, a ratings shift of just 1 percent for a prime-time program can mean a difference of $35 million per year to a network.

How does the A.C. Nielsen Company count the people watching each channel at each hour during each day? Just as a doctor can take a small blood sample to learn about all of a patient's blood, Nielsen samples a small percentage of America's televisions and uses that data to calculate what everyone else is probably watching. These samples are taken with electronic monitors placed in twelve hundred randomly selected homes and with program diaries that some one million volunteer families fill out. Nielsen claims its ratings are within 1.3 percent of perfect accuracy.

These program diaries also report such important demographic facts as the age, sex, and income of the audience members. If advertisers know these facts, they can avoid wasting money trying to sell razor blades to children, toys to adults, or detergent to men. Sometimes an advertiser will ignore a low rating if it is known that most of the audience is of the type most likely to buy a given product. A golf match, for example, may not attract many viewers, but the makers of golf clubs are eager to catch the eyes and ears of an audience made up almost entirely of golfers. Likewise, reruns of the science-fiction series "Star Trek" never had very high ratings, but Nielsen reported that its audience was generally young and financially well-off—just the type of people advertisers love to talk to.

Nielsen reports that America's peak viewing hours are between 8:00 p.m. and 10:00 p.m., that Sunday nights have the largest prime-time audience and Thursday nights have the smallest, and that older women watch the most and teen-age females watch the least. General drama shows are the most popular. Informational shows, such as news and documentaries, are the least popular. Four of the six most widely seen programs were Super Bowl games, and the largest audience in history watched the Apollo II moon voyage from July 14–27, 1969, when 93.9 percent of America was watching.

Networks, not the A.C. Nielsen Company, cancel shows with low ratings. When CBS announced its 1982–83 schedule, "Lou Grant" and "WKRP" were not on the list. Although both shows had won consistently high critical acclaim, ratings had dropped. In the case of "Lou Grant," a 32 audience share and 19.6 rating fell to 27 and 16.6—not high enough for prime time, when as many as 70 percent of America's television sets are turned on.

## PROBLEMS WITH RATINGS

Everyone has seen a favorite series canceled due to poor ratings, but the networks claim, quite correctly, that they are just trying to please as many people as possible, that they can't make everybody happy. The result of this goal, however, is programming aimed at pleasing a lot of people a little rather than a few people a lot.

Ratings fail to report what people would like to be watching and how much they like what they do watch. They do not report how many people are simply watching the programs they consider the least bad among what is available. They also do not report whether people are paying attention, or if they are developing negative attitudes about the programs, the networks, or the advertisers.

Many critics also question the mathematical accuracy of the ratings. The twelve hundred homes that A.C. Nielsen samples represent a mere .0003 percent of the American population. Furthermore, the monitors do not report who, if anyone, is actually watching the television. In one case, a woman confessed that she left the set on to entertain her dog. That dog erroneously represented the viewing habits of half a million Americans.

Additional problems with ratings are caused by the fact that the size of the audience depends on the time of day rather than the quality of the program. A program aired during prime time inevitably appears more popular simply because the available audience is larger.

The accuracy of the program diaries is also questioned. Although intended to enhance the data derived from the electronic monitors, the diaries may actually be confusing matters. Many families do not keep accurate records. Others lie in an attempt to keep their favorite shows on the air or because they are ashamed to admit they watched "Family Feud" instead of "The MacNeil/Lehrer Report."

Finally, after all these efforts and inaccuracies, the rankings mean little because the top ten programs are often almost equal. The margin of error involved in the calculations could completely rearrange the ranking.

## CONTROL OVER PROGRAMMING

Corporations, both advertisers and networks, have the strongest control over television programming. But they have neither total control over any one program nor partial control over all programs. The Federal government, through the Federal Communications Commission, also has some influence. Special interest groups, such as religious groups, ethnic groups, consumers, and parents can rally to exert pressure. The broadcast industry itself maintains self-control and ethical standards. But from time to time, any or all of these institutions can come into conflict, raising the essential question: Who should control programming?

In the early days of television, advertisers had almost total control over programming. They would buy entire time slots and then either produce their own shows or carefully oversee what the networks produced. By the 1960s, however, television time had become so expensive that only the largest corporations could afford to buy entire hours. This was a dangerous situation for smaller companies until ABC, then the smallest of the networks, invented the scatter plan. On ABC, and eventually on all networks, companies could buy half-minute segments on various shows rather than pay for entire shows.

With network time now available to hundreds of companies, none of them have the power to dictate the specific contents of the programs they sponsor. A network can afford to lose an advertiser that does not like what it is paying for. In a few cases, advertisers have tried to force networks to cancel shows. In 1972 Bumble Bee Tuna threatened to remove all advertising if CBS broadcast a congressional investigation of the fishing industry. CBS went ahead with the program, and Bumble Bee temporarily withdrew its advertisements. In 1979 General Electric protested when ABC's Barbara Walters scheduled an interview with Jane Fonda, who was bound to speak out against the nuclear power industry, one of G.E.'s biggest customers. G.E. withdrew sponsorship of the program; ABC aired it anyway.

Such instances are rare, however. More common is the subtle, unspoken cooperation between advertisers and broadcasters. A cartoon show sponsored by the makers of a sweet breakfast cereal would never have a hero express disgust over a non-nutritional breakfast. A police drama would never have the hero's car fail to start if its manufacturer was paying for the show and, incidentally, probably donating the car for the hero's use.

## THE POWER OF THE PEOPLE

A basic commandment of advertising is: "Thou Shalt Not Offend." An advertiser does not want to spend millions of dollars to make enemies. One off-color comment during prime time, in either an advertisement or a program, might incite hundreds of thousands of potential customers to purposefully avoid buying the advertiser's products.

(21)

If you had to say something to ninety-six million people of all ages, religions, and opinions without offending any of them, what would you talk about? Television writers and producers face that problem every day. Italians don't want all criminals to be from the Mafia. Mexican-Americans don't want to see ridiculously stereotyped Mexicans sleeping under sombreros. The American Medical Association doesn't want to see corrupt doctors or poor hospital care. The same applies to every race, religion, region, profession, sex, business, and belief in America.

Networks caution their writers about potential problems. As one writer put it, the guidelines for writing non-offensive scripts "leaves the writer with the freedom to write about nothing." This, say many critics, is what causes America's abundance of bland programming and repetitive plots.

The most widespread complaints from viewers and the general public are not about ethnic offenses but rather about the prevalence of violence and programs that use sexy stars in sexual situations to draw a large audience. In 1976 the National Citizens Committee for Broadcasting (NCCB) began publicizing the names of the most violent programs and their sponsors, urging people to watch other shows and buy other products. The Parent-Teacher Association endorsed the idea and the list and helped spread them across the country. Before a full-fledged boycott got underway, the J. Walter Thompson advertising agency, one of the largest in the country, advised its clients not to buy time on those programs. Not wanting to find themselves on a boycott list, the sponsors began moving their advertisements to other networks. The networks responded by toning down the violence, especially on cartoons and other children's shows.

Several other organizations have initiated similar boycotts, but their effects have been difficult to assess. In March 1982 the Coalition for Better Television and the Moral Majority announced a boycott against RCA, the owner of NBC, the network which they claimed had the most "un-Christian morals" in its programming. By the end of that year, RCA reported no change in the level of its sales, but the Moral Majority said the boycott had just begun.

These cases of viewers trying to exert pressure over television programming have had varied results, but it is clear that organized efforts can be effective. This new-found power carries inherent dangers, however. Demanding what should not be broadcast is just a step away from demanding what must be broadcast. If one special interest group ever managed to gain extensive control over television, other groups might find it difficult to express their opinions as persuasively and powerfully as those being beamed into eighty million homes. If that one group was successful enough, the one-sided weight of its opinion could be disastrous for democracy.

GOVERNMENT CONTROL:
THE FEDERAL
COMMUNICATIONS
COMMISSION

The First Amendment of the U.S. Constitution guarantees everyone's right to freedom of speech. Virtually every form of expression—books, art, movies, sermons, speeches, music—exist without any government control. The only exceptions are the mass media of radio and television, which are under the loose control of the Federal Communications Commission (FCC).

(23)

The seven-person board of the FCC was created to maintain technological order on the television and radio airwaves. It does this by issuing licenses and threatening to take them away if FCC regulations are not obeyed. While broadcasters appreciate the regulation of such technical matters as frequency and power of transmission, everyone is wary of the fact that government licensing is just a step away from government censorship. But the FCC makes it a point to keep its hands off programming. In the past fifty years, the FCC has refused to renew only 141 radio and television licenses out of the more than 70,000 it has issued.

Besides technical matters, the FCC uses its power to protect and enhance rather than control or inhibit freedom of speech. To keep the airways open to a diversity of programs and the opinions of more than just one or two giant companies, it prevents monopolies by limiting the number of stations one company can own and operate and by discouraging "cross-media" ownership of television stations and newspapers in the same town.

The FCC also takes the "public interest" into account when issuing and renewing licenses. This is as close as it comes to controlling programming, and it does so in three areas:

1. The Equal Time rule requires a station to let all political candidates have equal opportunities to express their views.

2. Obscenity rules forbid indecent language, nudity, and explicit sex.

3. The Fairness Doctrine requires stations to devote a reasonable amount of time to controversial public issues and to encourage the presentation of opposing ideas.

The FCC has been criticized both for being too lax and for being too strict. Many people say that it should exercise greater power in requiring stations and networks to act in the public interest by dealing with more important public issues and by broadcasting more educational and cultural shows. Others, fearing too much government control of this powerful medium, say that the demands of the market audience and the rules of capitalism are the fairest and most efficient ways of guiding and controlling the business of television in America.

In some democratic countries, the government has managed to release television from excessive control by government, business, and special interest groups. In England, the British Broadcasting System (BBC), the principal network of television and radio stations, is under nominal government control through a charter renewed by Parliament every five years. Its money comes from license fees paid by all owners of television and radio sets.

While the BBC's programming ranks among the best in the world, serious questions were raised during the Falklands War against Argentina in 1982. The British government was not only controlling war-news broadcasts but censoring and even distorting them as well. The supposed purpose of the incomplete or false information, which was never left incorrect for long, was to guard military secrets and uphold public morale. But some people felt that the government's virtual monopoly over the airwaves was being used as a propaganda tool aimed at sustaining public support for the war. The totalitarian government of Argentina was clearly using such a tactic to control its own people. The English government probably had no such self-serving intentions, but everyone was aware of the disturbing potential of government-controlled television.

## TELEVISION'S SELF-CONTROL

All-out competition can get out of hand very easily if there are no rules drawing the line between fair and unfair. Since the television industry is a competition among three networks and among the local stations in a given area, programming and advertising could easily become a free-for-all fight if the competitors had no standards of decent conduct. Responding to the popularity of violent shows, for example, the networks' efforts to gain the largest audience might escalate into programs of incredible blood and horror. The popularity of sexy stars could degenerate into pornography. The competition for advertising money could result in more commercial time than program time.

Although American television has never come close to such extremes, when the broadcasting industry was still young, the networks saw themselves beginning to move in that direction. They knew that if they went too far, the government would undoubtedly have to step in with strict regulations to keep programming and advertising within the limits of decency expected in American society.

Everyone prefers to live by their own rules rather than those of someone else. The networks and broadcasters decided that they could ward off the necessity of government control by enforcing self-control. The National Association of Broadcasters (NAB) was founded to bring together the members of the radio and television industries. Today, about 65 percent of all television broadcasters are NAB members. In 1952, in order to establish standards of conduct and keep NAB members from becoming irresponsible in their zeal to attract audience and advertisers, they adopted the Television Code.

The Television Code was a lengthy document with such sections as "Advancement of Education and Culture," "Responsibility Toward Children," and "Community Responsibility." Most of the standards and ideals mentioned were broad, vague, and easily ignored. But the section on "Special Program Standards," aimed specifically at preventing offensive or socially destructive programming, was clear and generally adhered to by broadcasters even though the NAB had no legal power over them. Some of the points of this section were precautions against ridiculing the handicapped, encouragement of sensitivity of the many races, beliefs, and ethnic origins of Americans, and a prohibition against advertisements for hard liquor, birth control devices, weapons, prescription drugs, and anything else that might be offensive or harmful to television viewers.

In 1976 the U.S. Justice Department ordered the NAB to stop enforcing all program standards, and in 1982 the NAB also eliminated all advertising standards after a federal court decided that some parts of the Television Code were violating antitrust laws by coordinating the networks as a unified monopoly. The court held that the Multiple Products Standard of the code, which prohibited advertising more than one product during any one commercial, was causing advertisers to pay more than they might otherwise, and thus causing increases in the prices of products. Other violations in the code were limits on the number of advertisements permitted per hour and per program. The NAB is appealing the decision, but until a higher court makes a final decision, the NAB is considering the Television Code nonexistent. No copies of it are available from the NAB, no records are kept of stations that fail to follow the code, and no efforts are made to admonish such stations. Most broadcasters are still following most points of the Television Code, however, because it has become a widely accepted standard over the last thirty years. Since the alternative to such self-control is government regulation, it is likely that the Television Code will continue as a general guideline for the broadcast industry.

# 4
# ADVERTISING

Almost 20 percent of all television broadcast time—one minute out of every five—is devoted to advertisements. In 1981 advertisers spent $8.2 billion on television, more than twice the combined national budgets of all Central American countries. Procter & Gamble alone spends half a billion dollars a year to show its household supplies to the American market. A commercial may cost $100,000 or more just to produce. Broadcasting it for thirty seconds during prime time can cost from $70,000 to $200,000. Imagine how many times you have seen a given commercial and you can imagine how much was spent to give you that message.

Is the expense worth the results? Advertisers are sure it is. On a simple dollars-per-viewer basis, television is the cheapest way to deliver a commercial message. In 1980 half a minute on "Happy Days" during prime time cost about $140,000, which came out to about half a cent per viewer. Thirty seconds during the 1980 Super Bowl went for $234,000, but the audience exceeded one hundred million, a cost of about one-quarter of a cent per person.

But television offers advertisers something beyond mass audience. The medium itself, with its unique ability to present coordinated sights, sounds, colors, and moving images, can grab, hold, and control an audience's attention in ways most people never know, even though they may see over twenty thousand hours of television commercials in a lifetime.

Since commercials can cost as much as $5,000 per second to broadcast, they are produced with exacting care. Teams of writers examine every word of the script. Lighting experts spend days creating the right mood for a certain scene. Actors are chosen after hundreds of auditions. An especially trusted personality may be paid more for a half-minute commercial than most Americans earn in ten years. The director of this thirty-second play may shoot the same scene dozens of times before every detail has been performed and recorded perfectly.

Behind each of these details are extensive experimental studies conducted by psychologists, sociologists, behavioral scientists, demographers, and marketing experts. Together they can determine what factors in a commercial will have certain predictable effects on the audience. They can test the effectiveness of a commercial by monitoring eye movements, pulse and perspiration rates, voice pitch, and even the brain waves of experimental viewers. After thousands of experiments, they know what factors—colors, music, types of characters, tones of voice, regional accents, number of camera shots, etc.—are the most persuasive to the types of people at whom the advertisement is aimed. They know, for example, that men pay attention to athletes and sexy women, that women tend to believe the voice of an authoritative male, and that characters from the Midwest are more credible than those from the Northeast. This is why a male audience may listen to a golfer selling tires, why a female audience will respect the opinion of an off-camera male telling a frustrated housewife how to clean her oven faster, and why the woman who is supposedly being secretly filmed giving her honest opinion about detergents is from Des Moines rather than from New York.

The goal of television advertising is not direct persuasion as much as simply putting an awareness of a product into the minds of potential customers and to have them associate, consciously or unconsciously, that product with something desirable. An ad for a children's game will stimulate a child's interest by showing Mom and Dad joining the fun. Some beer brewers show situations associating their brand with good times among friends. Cars are often associated with the freedom of open roads or with beautiful women. We all know that six-packs do not include a set of friends and that beautiful women are not among the options available at local car dealers. But when it comes time to buy one brand or another, these associations, reinforced by memories of clever songs and interesting sights, may be the deciding factors that clinch the final sale.

Most advertisers deny that they are doing much more than simply presenting information to the public. Sometimes this information comes as hard facts—price, calories, absorbency, miles per gallon, and so on. For other products, such as perfume or wine, the message is an emotion that allegedly accompanies the product. Advertisements that cannot offer hard facts make dubious claims about superior taste, cleanliness, freshness, style, speed of relief, and other factors that probably depend more on consumer preference than product quality. Television is an ideal advertising medium for such products. Hard facts can easily be put on the pages of magazines and newspapers, but when it comes to generating emotions and subjective preferences, you need sights, sounds, and action.

Whatever the approach of the advertisement, the advertisers naturally try to put their products in the best light possible. Fortunately, despite the scientific techniques, television advertisements are far from perfectly persuasive. Americans are not so obedient as to follow the orders of advertisers, and adults usually know better than to believe everything they see on television. Children and adolescents seem much more susceptible to advertising, however, and steps have been taken to protect them.

In the 1960s, when cigarette commercials were still allowed on television, one filterless brand claimed to "separate the men from the boys but not from the girls." Parents protested that cigarettes did neither and that this advertisement would prompt too many gullible teen-age boys to start smoking the strongest cigarettes in hopes of attaining maturity and sex appeal. The slogan was soon eliminated but its lesson remained. A few years later, in 1971, the Federal Trade Commission (FTC) banned all cigarette advertising from television in the hope that fewer people would start or continue smoking.

## CHILDREN AND ADVERTISING

Of special concern is the effect of television advertising on young children. The average preschooler sees some twenty-five thousand commercials per year. Still innocent of the ways of the world, children often go further than just believing that commercial cartoon characters are real. They often think that if they can get their parents to buy what these animated heroes are selling, they will win the love and friendship of the "people" they respect. While Tony the Tiger, for example, is apparently only asking kids to buy and eat his Frosted Flakes, innocent ears may be hearing a different message. They may think that Tony is real, that he is an expert on cereal, that he is honest in his appraisal and selection of cereals, that he will be their friend if they buy his brand, and that he might cry if they buy something else. An ad in a magazine would lack the reality of a moving, talking character and would not achieve this superpersuasive effect.

An advertiser that directly and explicitly said what Tony and his hundreds of colleagues imply would be considered guilty of false and deceptive advertising. The public would be outraged and the commercials would be banned. That children actually interpret commercials this way, regardless of the innocent intentions of advertisers, suggests that advertising for children may be inherently deceptive and therefore should be either banned or carefully controlled.

In 1970 Action for Children's Television (ACT), a watchdog organization that keeps an eye on children's programs, reported that nearly half the ads aimed at children are for foods, most of which are low in nutrition and high in sugar content. Others are for toys that, due to trick photography and misleading claims, are not nearly as much fun as they appear to be on television. ACT also pointed out commercials that are often in poor taste, such as one that showed a youngster experiencing the joy of slaughtering plastic soldiers with a toy machine gun.

In 1970 ACT petitioned the FCC to prohibit or at least control advertising on children's shows. They claimed that advertisements are actually a teach-and-learn experience for children who lack the maturity to analyze the truthfulness of what they see. The teachers in this video classroom are advertisers whose first concern is not the education of America's youngsters. Since children are intellectually defenseless under the influence of advertisers, ACT said, advertisements should be banned from children's programs.

Although the FCC did little in response, some one hundred thousand letters from concerned parents who were inspired by the petition hearings convinced drug companies to stop advertising vitamins as if they were candy. They also prompted networks to reduce commercial time on children's shows from sixteen minutes to the nine and a half minutes that are standard on most half-hour adult shows.

## HOW FREE IS TV?

Almost half of all Americans feel that most commercials are seriously misleading. Three-quarters of the public feel that there are too many advertisements on television. An equal percentage, however, feels that commercial interruptions are a reasonable price to pay for free entertainment.

But is it free? Who is paying the hundreds of millions of dollars it costs television producers to hire actors, destroy cars, blow up helicopters, travel around the world, and build miniature cities? Advertisers, by all appearances. But who is paying the hundreds of millions of dollars it costs to have Morris the Cat tell us about cat food or Mr. Whipple expound on the virtues of squeezable toilet paper?

By buying advertised products, American consumers are paying for the advertisements that pay for the television shows. American television is not free. Consumers are willing to pay as much as 18 percent more for products they recognize from advertisements they have seen on television. They simply assume that the products are superior because they have been televised. Consumers pay the manufacturers of the products and the manufacturers' advertisements pay the television producers. Cartoons are paid for by the slightly heightened price of sweet cereals; baseball players' salaries are paid in part by the price of canned shaving cream and radial tires; soap operas are paid for by the price of cleansers and detergents. Consequently, an average family pays as much as $200 a year in these indirect costs—whether or not they watch television.

If manufacturers are willing to spend millions on advertising and consumers are willing to pay more for advertised products, then advertising is successfully reaching from one end of the economic system to the other. It is, in fact, an important factor in the success of twentieth-century capitalism. As economist John Kenneth Galbraith wrote in *The New Industrial State*, "The industrial system is profoundly dependent upon commercial television and could not exist in its present form without it. . . . radio and television are the prime instruments for the management of consumer demand." Through advertising, especially television advertising, manufacturers can usually generate enough sales to pay the start-up costs of creating a new product, mass producing it, and distributing it to the shelves and showrooms of American retailers. The assurance that the products will sell makes it easier for companies to take the investment risk of introducing new products to the market and expanding into new areas of business. Advertising is important to the growth of business, and that growth is essential to the health of the capitalist economy of modern America.

# 5

## TELEVISION AND PEOPLE

In Jerzy Kosinski's novel *Being There*, the hero grew up within the confines of a single house and its garden. Until adulthood, he never experienced the outside world except through his television. Eventually, when thrown into the real world—actually "being there" rather than just seeing it on television—he could act and react with other people only as he had seen it done in the artificial world of television. People considered him an intelligent man and an ideal American, and he soon became a candidate for president. *Being There* is only an allegory, but its moral is a very important message about how television may be affecting people.

## MARSHALL McLUHAN

Marshall McLuhan, a Canadian professor of communication, was among the first to point out the extraordinary powers of the electronic media that pervade modern society. Without labeling mass media as good or bad, he warned the world that civilization is undergoing a change more rapid and radical than any in history.

In *Understanding Media: The Extensions of Man*, McLuhan described the progress of civilization as resulting from the gradual extension of the human body. Spears and atomic bombs are extensions of the fist because they help us fight from a distance. Wheels and wings are extensions of the foot because they help us transport ourselves and our things farther and faster than we can walk. Books are an extension of the eyes and ears because they help us receive information about times and places too distant to see or hear. And the electronic media, especially television, are the ultimate extension of not only the eye and ear but also the central nervous system since information can be transmitted from a television camera's "eye" to the viewer's brain in less than a second. With television, our eyes and ears have extended from a radius of a few hundred yards to the other side of the world and, with the cameras aboard the *Voyager* spacecraft, even to the other side of the solar system.

Civilization has gone through three stages, according to Marshall McLuhan. In the preliterate or tribal stage, primitive people knew only what they actually saw or heard, usually within the confines of their own village and its locale. They needed no great powers of thought to learn what was happening because the events were right there to be seen or heard.

In the literate or post-tribal stage, people could learn from books rather than from actual experience. With the relatively sophisticated and active thought that reading demands, one could learn about events in other places and times without actually being there to see or hear them happen.

Today, in McLuhan's third stage, postliterate or retribalized civilization, modern man communicates and learns in much the same way as primitive man. Through television, we once again learn by seeing and hearing what happens in our "village." We do not have to think actively in order to learn about events because the television set presents them for easy seeing and hearing. There is an important difference from the original tribal stage, however. Our modern village is the entire planet and its history. McLuhan calls this "the global village," and points out that it has been built in just the last fifty of the five hundred thousand years of human existence. The effects of mass media on mankind and society are by no means understood, but they are undeniably present and powerful.

Marshall McLuhan is most famous for creating a very complex and profound concept which he condensed into five words: "The medium is the message." Every message contains information, he said, and every message is transmitted through a medium, be it sign language, speech, print, television, or any of the many other ways of communicating information. But the message received may have more, less, or different information from the message that was sent. This modification of information occurs in the medium that transmits it.

In the case of television, any message sent takes on an appearance of importance simply because it is on television. If you gave a speech on a soapbox in the park, for example, you would be ignored or ridiculed by most of the people walking by. If you gave that exact same speech on network television, people would pay attention and would think your ideas worth considering, or at least worth arguing about. The only difference between the two speeches is the medium that carried them to the audience, yet the two audiences heard quite different messages.

Advertisers appreciate and are quite willing to pay for the importance that television gives their messages. Magazine advertisements, packages, and posters in stores often say "As advertised on TV!" in order to lend greater importance to the product. Political candidates also know that they must appear on television if they want the respect of voters. News broadcasters know they carry a special responsibility because their audiences will assume that what is reported is the most important news and that what is not reported is not worthy of public attention.


## SOCIALIZATION

Understanding Dr. McLuhan's abstract ideas is relatively simple compared to the task of understanding the down-to-earth effects of television on people. To understand how television influences society, we must first understand how society influences individuals.

Through the process of socialization, we all learn how to behave in society by observing the behavior of others. Just as aborigine children grow up to share the values, language, dialect, beliefs, and general culture of the other members of their tribe, children in Chicago or Hong Kong tend to take on the cultural characteristics of the society that surrounds them.

Before the twentieth century and the advent of the mass media that would allow millions of people to share an identical experience, the socialization process in America involved relatively small groups of people. One's family served as the primary example of how people were supposed to behave. Boys learned from their fathers how a man should behave; girls learned their roles in life from their mothers. The peers one met at school, work, and church would add other information to one's lessons on how to be normal and to fit into society. Consequently, such factors as geography, religion, and social class would determine to a great extent one's values and how one would behave in the myriad situations that confront everyone sooner or later in life.

Today, with television in the homes of virtually every American family, socialization may have taken on a radically new aspect. At the turn of a dial, the poor can peek into middle-class living rooms, children can witness the drama of war, and families can experience the excitement of cops and robbers, cowboys and Indians, Frankenstein and Godzilla. Through the television, we see— or assume we see—how doctors, police, business people, single parents, rich families, foreign diplomats, and countless other types of people behave. And we may assume that this is the proper way to behave in the real world.

## THE NEW NORMALITY

All this adds up to more than simple entertainment. Since American families spend more time watching television than doing any other single activity except sleeping, working, or going to school, we are, in terms of time, paying more attention to video heroes than to our families and friends. When spending so much time with these fictional characters in their fictional situations, Americans may be learning ways of behaving. Our perceptions of normal behavior may be coming from the place where we have focused our attention.

The population of the video world is quite different from the population that watches it. The most constant viewers are the elderly, the poor, ethnic minorities, and women. Most of the people they see on television, however, tend to be young, middle-class, white, and male. Characters that do not have at least three of these characteristics are relatively rare. Those with major roles in soap operas, cartoons, dramas, and commercials are usually presented as ideal people—handsome, intelligent, educated, and well employed.

Women, who make up less than a third of the television population, tend to be unemployed and either dependent on a man or without any visible means of support, although recently there has been an increase in women who manage to be both professionals and motherly housewives. In all, women make up about 20 percent of the labor force on television while in the real world they are almost half of America's labor force. On television, just five occupations—nurse, secretary, entertainer, maid, and model—employ half the television women. Men are seen in a much wider variety of occupations and also in more authoritative positions. According to a survey in 1974, over 57 percent of television men were employed in upper management or high-ranking law enforcement or government positions. Only 28 percent of the women had such jobs.

The portrayal of blacks on television has changed significantly over the past fifteen years. Before the civil rights movement of the 1960s, the few blacks on television were always in stereotyped subservient positions. They were never seen in commercials. Today, however, they are only slightly less prevalent on television than in American society. Their social position on television is substantially better, too. Most television blacks are employed and their presence in managerial and professional jobs is much higher than is really the case. They constitute 7 percent of television's criminals and 27 percent of the victims of crime, in both cases much below the actual national average.

Television representation of the economic classes is very disproportionate in comparison with the situation in contemporary America. Most employed people on television have jobs with high income and high social prestige—doctors, lawyers, businesspeople, and so on. Law enforcement is by far the most common occupation on television. Blue-collar workers such as trade and factory workers are scarce on television although in reality they are the largest portion of America's labor force.

What are the consequences of television misrepresenting the makeup of society? Psychologists and sociologists are just beginning to study this complex question. Several experiments in the 1970s found that adults tend to modify their behavior in imitation of what they see on television. When what they saw was different from what society prescribes as normal or proper, however, social pressure usually had the stronger influence. For example, females who watched programs with aggressive heroes did not become significantly more aggressive because according to social rules and tradition, women are not supposed to be aggressive. Men who saw those same shows, however, quickly assumed more aggressive traits.

A study of people who watch soap operas indicated that people's perceptions of the real world are influenced by what they see on television. On soap operas, virtually all important characters are upper-middle class with white-collar jobs. The problems they face are always on a personal level, never involving national politics or social ills. Most of these problems can be cured by doctors, lawyers, or psychiatrists. Contrary to reality, homicide is the chief cause of death, and women suffer from cardiovascular disease four times more often than men. In the experiment, a group of television viewers were ranked according to how much time they spent watching soap operas. Then they were asked such questions as what percent of Americans are murdered, divorced, have been in jail, are doctors, and are in the upper-middle class. The results showed that the more people watched soap operas, the more their answers were true for what they saw on television rather than what is true in the real world.

The implications, not yet verified but considered worth extensive experimentation, reach far beyond soap operas and their audience. Quite possibly, if we unconsciously assume that what we see on television is normal, we may modify our behavior in the real world according to what would be right in the television world. The effects could be either positive or negative. In the case of blacks commonly portrayed as equals in social and professional situations, television might help to eliminate prejudice in the real world. On the other hand, women portrayed as either unemployed housewives or superefficient working mothers might cause people to expect too much or too little of women. It will take years of experimentation to determine to what extent, if any, these possible effects are actually happening.

# VIDEO VIOLENCE

When the Secret Service began interrogating John W. Hinckley, Jr., after his attempted assassination of President Reagan in 1981, the young man had a question for his interrogators: "Is it on TV?"

For months before, Mr. Hinckley had been alone, watching endless hours of television, which he later called a dangerous practice that leads to dangerous fantasies. His fantasy led him to collect handguns and dream of having the prestige of the president with a bulletproof vest, bodyguards, a helicopter, and plenty of television coverage. On March 30, 1981, John Hinckley fulfilled his fantasy quickly and violently, and people wonder how much of his insanity was absorbed from a television set.

No aspect of television concerns the American public as much as the prevalence of violence on television and its possible effects on television viewers. During prime time, a violent incident occurs five times every hour, and on Saturday mornings, it flares to eighteen times per hour. Seventeen percent of all television characters are law enforcers, and 60 percent of all crime victims are murdered. All this adds up to more violence in a day of television than most people experience in a lifetime.

What is the nature of video violence? It is quite different from watching a couple of kids slug it out in a playground. On television, the fight is usually between a hero and a criminal or a victim and a criminal. When Magnum or the S.W.A.T. team resort to violence, as they inevitably do, it is clear who is wrong and who is right; that the right have good reason to fight, and that in the end, the right will win.

How does this simplistic view of violent conflict affect people who watch it day after day? An experiment comparing children who watch a lot of violent programs to children who watched only nonviolent programs revealed that children of the former group were more likely to agree that "It's OK to hit someone if you are mad at them for a good reason," just as they have seen their heroes do again and again on television. Children in the second group, on the other hand, had apparently learned that problems can often be solved passively, through discussion or appeal to an authority.

Video violence also gives a distorted view of what violence involves. After a few shots fired by Kojak, for example, the problem is solved and forgotten. There is no discussion of the fundamental cause of the crime, the blood and suffering of either the innocent victims of crime or the "deserving" criminal, or of the long-term effects of the incident. We never know why an individual is resorting to crime. Perhaps poverty or a bad family life were the reasons. We don't see the shooting victim, guilty or innocent, writhing with the agony of a bullet in the chest, and we don't see the condition of that victim months later when he or she may still be mentally or physically crippled. Nor do we see the family at the funeral or how their lives will change as a result of the violence. Video violence is quick, clean, easy and, within an hour, forgotten.

Whether television should depict these very real aspects of violence is a debatable point. Some say it would be in bad taste to bring blood, gore, and misery into American living rooms. Others feel that ignoring these parts of violence desensitizes viewers by making it look painless, inconsequential, and all too easy to commit. A child may grow up thinking that pulling a trigger results in nothing more than a bang and an easy end to the problem. But guns are not like that, and neither is life.

Violence reaches further absurdity on Saturday mornings. When several pounds of dynamite explode in Wylie Coyote's hand, he escapes with minor cuts and bruises that heal and disappear before the end of the next commercial. When Thundarr the Barbarian defeats his foes on what ACT has rated the most violent program on the air, with as many as seventy-eight violent incidents per hour, it is Thundarr, not the law or government, who has decided what is right or wrong. Such civilized concepts as a trial and just punishment never enter the picture.

Does violence on television actually create violence in the real world? There have been a few incidents of children and adults imitating what they saw on television. A seven-year-old boy was caught sprinkling glass in his family's stew because he wanted to see if it had the same effects he saw on television. Two Chicago boys tried to extort some money by using a bomb-threat scheme they had seen on television. In California a girl was raped with a broomstick as had happened the night before on an NBC program, an incident that provoked an unsuccessful lawsuit against that network. But these occurrences of imitative violence are scarce. What really concerns people are the attitudes that television violence may be instigating.

In 1972 the U.S. Surgeon General, who is responsible for overseeing the general health of the American public, issued a report that clearly linked violence on television to generally violent behavior. Due to the problems of performing accurate studies, the report was considered somewhat unsubstantial and inconclusive. In

1982, however, a report by the National Institute of Mental Health, entitled *Television and Behavior: Ten Years of Scientific Progress*, clearly concluded that there is "overwhelming" evidence that "excessive" violence on television causes violent behavior in children. Some of the evidence used in the study indicated that children who watch a lot of violent programs are more likely to be aggressive during play, to accept force as a solution to problems, and to fear becoming a victim of violence.

Other studies have indicated that adults who watch a lot of television violence may have an increased tendency to become violent. They may also share an exaggerated fear of evil in the world. They tend to overestimate the extent and seriousness of crime in America, and they have a greater fear that other people will try to take advantage of them. Taking this fear a step further, some historians have noted that when the people of a given society are afraid, they are easier to lead. In the past, generalized paranoia has often resulted in a dictatorship that uses the fear and the support of the people to assume extraordinary powers that rarely serve the betterment of that society. More often, the result is a restriction of civil liberties in the name of law and order, or a military buildup and subsequent war in the name of national security. Could the fear that is generated by television ever have such results in America? It is impossible to predict but well worth remembering in the future.

Why so much violence on television? While some are saying that television is creating the increase of violence in America, others claim that television is merely mirroring the realities of America and helping to express the concerns of Americans.

A more likely explanation is that violence is a very

basic plot technique that writers and producers use to stimulate their audiences. It takes little depth of thought or development of character personalities. An exciting fight is guaranteed to capture an audience. Pulses quicken, sweat glands open, muscles tighten, and viewers willingly sit through the commercials in order to see what happens in the end.

Violence is also one of the few subjects producers do not fear will offend and lose audiences, which is what happens when controversial subjects are used in drama. Drama needs conflict, but when the conflict involves serious questions about race, religion, politics, and other issues about which many people disagree, a large segment of the audience may become angry and turn the channel. In some cases, affiliate stations have refused to clear programs considered too controversial in their local areas. Networks therefore avoid such controversial subjects, and the only conflict left is violence. As long as the good guys win, the audience seems reasonably content.

A few programs manage to create conflict without killing. Michael Landon, who is both star and executive director of "Little House on the Prairie," tries to put moral lessons in his show in an attempt to teach while entertaining. On "Hill Street Blues," the conflicts are usually personal and political matters among the characters. Although some violence does occur, the theme is not the action but rather its consequences. "M*A*S*H," too, has been successful in portraying the results of violence without showing the actual killing. The success of such shows indicates that a large part of the American audience appreciates nonviolent conflict. If ratings continue to indicate a popular demand for these types of programs, the networks will probably create more like them.

# SEX

Compared to the content of many books, magazines, and movies, sex on television is in reasonably good taste. Compared to what a large part of American society has traditionally accepted as moral and normal, however, television is coming closer to lewdness every year. Subjects such as rape, incest, infidelity, and homosexuality, which were taboo twenty years ago, are becoming commonplace. During prime time, prostitutes are more common than plumbers. During afternoon soap operas, sex between unmarried partners is almost ten times more common than for married couples. Even on Saturday mornings, animated heroines are often depicted as young, sexy, and not rarely wearing thigh-high skirts or skintight leotards.

All these aspects of sex on television are providing the American child with early and easy access to information that used to be reserved for adults. This information is not explicit, technical, or terribly accurate, but it is ubiquitous in various shades of subtlety. In advertisements, Ultra-brite toothpaste offers sex appeal, Sergio Valente offers close-ups of posteriors, and Sprite offers tan blondes on the beach. On drama shows, Charlie's Angels and Wonder Woman often fight crime with bikinis and wet shirts. During "The Tonight Show," when an estimated one million children are still watching television, the majority of the jokes are based on sex. Even some game shows, such as "The Newlywed Game" and "The Match Game," use sexual innuendo to keep an audience's interest. Sex on television may not be as vivid as violence, but the subject seems uppermost in the minds of the people on the screen.

But sex appeal is no reason to buy toothpaste; law enforcement officers do not wear bikinis; and prostitutes are not more common than plumbers. Just as with subjects mentioned earlier, like violence, television has created an unreal world where sex has an enhanced importance while other matters are banished from apparent existence.

How does the presentation of sex affect television viewers? Psychologists and sociologists know less about this than about violence. Some suspect that viewers may be comparing their own lives with the lives of the eternally beautiful people who, during prime time, implicitly engage in premarital and extramarital sex seven times more often than in normal marital relations. Soap operas are even more heavily oriented to sex. According to a study reported in *The Journal of Communications* in 1980, "General Hospital," the most popular soap opera among adult women and teen-agers, was also the sexiest, exhibiting an average of sixteen incidents of sexual behavior per hour.

Apparently television sex does not tantalize as much as make certain moral values look normal. Constant viewers may begin to feel that what goes on during prime time is going on in real life as well, that it is proper behavior or that society is more depraved than it appears. This may cause them to modify their behavior. One study indicated that incidents of teen-age pregnancy were more common among young women who watched a lot of television. Another study concluded that adolescents who watch a lot of television have higher and distorted expectations of "what sex should be like."

Television certainly is not the primary driving force behind the changing sexual mores in America. To the contrary, television, to a large extent, is just reflecting social changes that have already occurred. What disturbs many people is that these changes appear more extreme and widespread on television and that they are being shown to children as if they were adults.

Scientists have just begun studying the relationships between television and people. They know that they are interactive, that what happens on television influences society, and that what happens in society influences what is on television. The question is how it happens and to what extent. The answer is a hard one to grasp because people as individuals, society as a whole, and television as a mass medium are changing continuously. Only after scientists have established a substantial body of facts about these ever-changing factors will we be able to knowledgeably approach the question of what, if anything, to do about television in America.

# 6
# TELEVISION AND CHILDREN

The youngest bank robber in history was a nine-year-old boy who carried a toy gun into a New York City bank, made a credible threat, and walked out with $118. He didn't get far, though, and soon found himself in court. His lawyer opened his defense by saying that the boy had been victimized by television, that "a steady diet of TV caused a malnutrition of values."

In previous chapters we discussed the effects of television sex, violence, and advertising on children. These are the most obvious and directly negative ways that television may be influencing children's behavior. But television may be producing other effects as well, some more subtle and some more positive. The subtle effects of children spending more time watching television than on any other activity may be the intellectual equivalent of eating nothing but cookies and potato chips. On the other hand, educational television and the tremendous amount of information that television in general brings to children may prove that the medium has beneficial potentials that the industry has only just begun to explore.

## THE PLUG-IN DRUG

In a book entitled *The Plug-In Drug*, author Marie Winn expresses some concerns shared by many American parents. The principal danger, she says, is not what is on television but rather the amount of time children spend watching it. She fears that they are inadvertently learning to passively absorb experience and information without actually doing anything. Since they are not reading, writing, or conversing, their language abilities suffer. Since television offers instant entertainment, they are less likely to play games, read books, do chores, make friends, build things, explore the world around them, or participate in any of the other activities that help children develop into social, active, intellectual adults. Marie Winn also thinks that television hurts family life by causing people to focus their lives around the television instead of around each other.

So far, there are no widely accepted studies to support or dispute these claims, though such suspicions are what lead to such studies. Like most questions about the effects of television on people, they are hard, if not impossible, to answer.

## EDUCATIONAL TELEVISION

In 1967 the Public Broadcasting System created the Children's Television Workshop (CTW) and began planning America's first children's educational television program. In the existing field of cartoons and other kids' shows, CTW had nothing to copy from to generate ideas.

The challenge was to find a way to teach people who had notoriously short attention spans and the freedom to change channels at will. The answer to the challenge was "Sesame Street," which was first broadcast in November, 1968.

Imagine trying to be a teacher without knowing who is present or absent, who is asleep or attentive, who is bored with simple lessons or confused by hard lessons. CTW decided to use some basic advertising techniques to keep the audience's attention. "Sesame Street's" messages are short, easy to grasp, often repeated, and without logical continuity from one message to the next. Quick camera shots and lots of action keep interest at a peak. Plenty of puppets, clowns, and cartoons create the fun that makes the children want to learn. With no punishment for failure and no humiliation for getting an answer wrong, there is little to discourage children. If a particular lesson gets too boring, within moments it is finished and replaced with a new subject being demonstrated by new characters in a new situation. Under such optimum learning conditions, the pupils tend to stay around for more fun and more information.

This teaching strategy may have inherent drawbacks, however. In adapting to a child's short attention span, programs like "Sesame Street" do little to encourage concentration. When the children get to school, they may find it all the harder to work on a given project long enough to achieve anything. They may expect all lessons to last only a minute and to be repeated several times. From the child's point of view, the classroom, without puppets and cartoons, may be a monotonous place to learn.

Educational programs deliver information in two ways. "Sesame Street" and "The Electric Company,"

(55)

aiming at the preschool audience, concentrate on such academic areas as letters, numbers, and geometrical shapes. They also present skits that demonstrate such skills as the ability to recognize, classify, detect relationships, and think rationally. It is hoped that the development of these skills will help children learn faster after they get to school.

"Mister Rogers' Neighborhood," another product of Children's Television Workshop, has the more subtle goal of teaching healthy social behavior. Without lecturing or preaching, puppets, clowns, cartoons and skits are always exhibiting some form of altruism, cooperation, courage, kindness, or toleration. Characters of various races and nationalities get along with each other like brothers and sisters. Studies have shown that children tend to imitate and identify with these model characters. The people of CTW are proud to tell the story of a young black boy who was watching "Mister Rogers" when he pointed to the screen and said, "Look! He looks like me and he knows the answer!" Obviously the boy was learning something far more important than a letter of the alphabet.

How well do these shows fulfill their purported functions? Studies of their effects on children have not been in complete agreement but a generally accepted conclusion is that most children do learn something from "Sesame Street" and "The Electric Company" if they watch regularly. Children from lower economic classes seem to learn less, probably because the lessons are not reinforced by parents. Children who watch with a parent or teacher and then discuss what they saw, or play games provided by CTW, learn the most of all. In general, regular viewers do better in the first and second grade, though after that the other children catch up. This final fact may be the most important because if it is true, it means that "Sesame Street" and "The Electric Company" are accomplishing little more than giving children a few extra facts which they would have learned in school anyway. Of course, it might also mean that the schools are not taking advantage of the education that the children have before the first day of the first grade. Also, the children may be too used to the action-packed lessons they saw on television. Such debatable points will not be cleared up for some time to come.

Studies have also indicated that children who watch these shows, especially "Mister Rogers' Neighborhood," seem to learn good social behavior. In one experiment, one group of children watched a few hours of "Mister Rogers" while another watched violent shows. When observed in play, the children of the first group were friendlier and more cooperative. The second group tended to be aggressive, violent, and antisocial.

Despite these apparently successful results, educational television is not without its critics. In 1971 the British Broadcasting System banned "Sesame Street" from its programming schedule. Monica Simms, then head of BBC's children's television department, expresed doubts that children shoud be learning in a passive, uninvolved way, as they do with television. She was also concerned about "Sesame Street's" lack of reality, its portrayal of middle-class life without reference to lower-class life, and its attempts to prepare children for school but not for life. She was also worried about "Sesame Street's" admitted goal of modifying children's behavior, which she felt was a form of authoritarian indoctrination and a dangerous use of television.

Such criticisms have been rare and not based on conclusive scientific studies. In general, regardless of doubts, most parents and educators feel that PBS's programs are by far preferable to the alternatives on commercial networks.

## ACTION FOR
## CHILDREN'S TELEVISION

Action for Children's Television (ACT) was formed by a group of parents who were concerned about what their children were watching on television. ACT monitors children's shows, rates them according to levels of violence, informs the public of its findings, gives advice on controlling children's viewing habits, and petitions the FCC to require networks to improve the quality of children's programs. As we have seen in Chapter Four, ACT also analyzes children's commercials to see if advertisers are using deceptive techniques.

Despite the fact that young children watch more television than any other age group, there are very few shows produced just for them. ACT points out that "Captain Kangaroo" is the only regular weekday children's show on a commercial network, and even that was recently cut to half an hour. What remain are the Saturday morning cartoons, most of which are either extremely violent or, at best, not dealing with any socially constructive subjects. Among the few shows that ACT considers good enough for children are "Schoolhouse Rock," "Fat Albert and the Cosby Kids," "Special Treat," "In the News," and all the children's programs broadcast on PBS. ACT announces Achievement Awards for good children's programs. So far ABC has won four, CBS has won seven, NBC one, and PBS thirteen.

ACT has been pressing the FCC to alleviate this situation. In 1971 the FCC set up a children's television unit to study the problem. In 1974 the FCC's *Children's Television Report and Policy Statement* emphasized that broadcasters had a special obligation to "present programming that would serve the unique needs of the child audience." The report specified certain standards concerning the amount, type, age of audience, and scheduling of programs that broadcasters should respect. By 1978, however, broadcasters had made few changes. In response to an ACT petition, the FCC established the Children's Television Task Force to investigate the problem. It found that broadcasters had failed to meet their obligation to improve children's programming. The FCC then proposed regulations, but they were never put into effect. In October 1980 the FCC held hearings in which various types of child-development specialists, members of the television industry, and ACT all urged the FCC to require children's programming on weekdays. Summing up the decade of talk and investigation, FCC Chairman Charles Ferris said, "Should we wait another ten years? Will too many generations of children be lost?"

Three weeks after Ferris's statement, Ronald Reagan was elected president and an antiregulation mood took control in Washington. Mark Fowler, newly appointed FCC chairman, agreed with the president that the FCC should "get out of the way" of free enterprise. For the immediate future, therefore, no new regulations are expected. In fact, Chairman Fowler wants to remove the words "public interest" from the Communications Act which created the FCC and which have guided the television industry since its birth. This would allow broadcasting to act as any other industry providing its "customers" with what they want, not necessarily what is best for them.

ACT has now adopted the tactic of mobilizing public opinion. In their newsletters they urge parents to write to advertisers, networks, and government representatives. Besides their Achievement Awards and ratings of violent shows, they rank networks and advertisers in order of televised and sponsored violence. By prompting parents to avoid violent shows and the products of their sponsors, ACT hopes to affect ratings and profits just enough to force networks to change their programming and advertisers to seek less violent shows.

ACT also advises parents on how to control their children's viewing habits. They suggest that parents watch with their children so they can discuss the differences betwen reality and television, how television characters could solve problems without using violence, how advertised foods are often unhealthy, and how advertised toys may not be as good as they look on television. ACT also suggests that parents control television time and encourage their children to plan what they will watch, to keep the dial on PBS as much as possible, and to turn the set off as soon as a program ends.


BENEFICIAL EFFECTS
OF TELEVISION

It is very easy to point out the negative effects of television. Most studies and experiments have been searching for the antisocial ways that television hurts society by negatively affecting children. But there are also pro-social effects that contribute to society. Television is the most powerful teaching tool ever devised. Unfortunately, in most cases it has not been intended to teach and therefore its lessons are all too often wrong, misleading, or downright damaging. But television also brings home some basic lessons in everything from geography to social behavior.

Beyond any doubt, television is a window on a world so vast and varied that a human being can witness only the slightest fraction of it all. With television, Jacques Cousteau shows us sharks in the Mediterranean, National Geographic shows us llamas in the Andes, and Carl Sagan shows us everything from the insides of atoms to the fringes of the universe. Teachers and books can do the same thing—and nothing can ever replace them—but television offers one more way for children to explore without actually traveling. Even without watching documentaries, children can see the inside of an airplane cockpit, the engine room of a submarine, the rigging of an old sailing ship, a ranch in the Midwest, the inside of a police station, and the major capitals of the world. Prime-time programs may not be presenting thorough lessons on such subjects, but by the time the child grows up, he or she has at least glimpsed such things and is ready to really learn about them.

In terms of social behavior and morality, all that television portrays is not bad. In fact, most of it is good. There is plenty of violence, but the good guys always win, and the children who see it, while perhaps becoming more prone to violent behavior, at least are learning something about the difference between good and bad. Hard work, perseverance, courage, and kindness are usually depicted as desirable traits that result in some sort of reward. Drugs are never glorified and heavy drinkers are, at best, buffoons. Parents are loving and involved with their children, and the children respect and obey their parents. Professionals and working people are either ethical and good at their jobs or else play the antagonist in a conflict they will lose. All these typical television situations are subtle lessons that children pick up and, it is hoped, believe and practice later in life.

Dr. Jerome L. Singer, a psychology professor at

Yale University, was an advisor for the National Institute for Mental Health's 1982 report on the effects of television which was mentioned in Chapter Five. After the public paid so much attention to the negative effects that the report had established, Dr. Singer pointed out that the report had also found a potential for positive, constructive effects. Experiments had shown that television could teach children such prosocial behavior as cooperation, sharing, and taking turns. In one experiment, for example, children who watched a child on television showing affection for a doll later showed increased affection for dolls. In another experiment, children saw a child win money in a game. The child then donated the money to a charity and received a reward and kind words from an adult. When the subjects of the experiment were put in a similar situation, they did the same. Commercial television was found to have prosocial effects when a survey of children between the ages of seven and ten who watched "Fat Albert and the Cosby Kids" revealed that 90 percent of them understood at least one message about the right way to behave in society.

Dr. Singer also said that television can foster better health attitudes, such as not smoking. Unfortunately, he noted, television programming has not been constructed to utilize these capabilities. He suggested that the value of television could be enhanced if children were taught the skill of how to watch television just as they are taught how to read a novel or a newspaper. Therefore, some of the negative aspects of television may be partially the fault of parents and schools.

Television is only one of many factors that influence the socialization process. Parents, peers, siblings, neighbors, churches, and schools all contribute to the character of a growing child. In fact, these real people and institutions are much more influential than television. Television certainly affects children, but the surrounding family and community either counter-affect or reinforce what television teaches. For example, if a child sees violence on television but in church hears about turning the other cheek, in school is told not to fight, and at home lives with loving parents, the violence on television will probably have little or no effect. But if the child never goes to church, gets involved in fights in school, and sees his parents argue with each other, the violence on television may be reinforced by the social values evident in the real world. Apparently television has the potential for both good and bad effects, but it does not act alone; society remains far more influential.

# 7

## TELEVISION AND THE TRUTH

Every evening, fifty-six milion people in 40 percent of American homes watch the evening news. This is more than the number of people who read newspapers. Polls indicate that 51 percent of Americans consider television news more honest and reliable than any other form of news media. Television is America's primary news source, and just as any other news medium, it influences the opinions that guide the American democracy.

This is not to say that the networks are purposefully trying to control what U.S. citizens see and think. Quite the contrary, the networks, in general, have maintained very high journalistic standards in bringing their audiences neutral, balanced reports. But the nature of television as a means of reporting news has certain limitations and characteristics that unavoidably influence people and their opinions. Radio, newspapers, and magazines also have limitations inherent to their means of delivering the news. But none of these media are as widely seen and believed as television.

The greatest power of the television news report is its unique ability to actually show the viewer what is happening virtually anywhere in the world. If a picture is worth more than ten thousand words, a thirty-minute news report contains the information of several newspapers, magazines, and books. For example, reading about civilian casualties in the beseiged Beirut of 1982, barely compared with seeing the blood, the homeless people running from explosions, and the Palestinian guerrillas and Israeli soldiers firing machine guns on city streets. During the 1960s and 1970s, television literally brought home the Vietnam war as American families watched the action, live and in color, as it happened in jungle combat zones. During the hostage crisis in Iran from 1979 to 1981, Americans could see their imprisoned compatriots, the angry mobs outside the U.S. embassy, and the charred bodies of the American soldiers who died in the aborted rescue mission. Such scenes displayed in living rooms cannot help but stir emotions and influence the opinions of the people who watch them.

This great power of television news relates directly to one of its greatest weaknesses. The limits of a thirty-minute time slot and the limited availability of camera crews mean that a lot of news, indeed most of it, cannot be shown. The Associated Press (AP) and United Press International (UPI), the two largest news agencies that write and sell reports to newspapers and radio and television stations, file a total of over five million words of news every day. That's a lot of news, and only the tiniest fraction of it gets broadcast on television. Most people never hear about the rest and those who get all their news from the networks tend to assume that they have seen and heard the essential events, if not all the events, that have happened on planet earth since the day before. But they have not. They have seen only that which the networks have decided is most important and, quite often, that which television cameras have managed to catch. News producers recognize this responsibility and have done their best not to ignore important events. Former CBS anchorperson Walter Cronkite, long considered the best newscaster on television, admitted that his and other news programs were only a glance at headlines, rarely a deep or complete report of the news of the world. Nevertheless, he and other news announcers usually sign off by saying something to the effect of "And that's the news around the world."

Time limit is not the only factor governing the news that most Americans get to see. Since television is so good at showing action, that is what viewers expect and that is what news producers strive to provide. Terrorism, tornadoes, riots, wars, and other disasters are the best subjects for good film footage. There is plenty for the audience to look at. But how do you film the gradual rusting of a major bridge, the writing of a congressional bill, or the merger of major corporations? Such events may have important ideas behind them and long-term effects ahead of them, but ideas and effects need explanations, not film footage. Networks need large audiences to pay the tremendous expense of collecting international news, and they know that a bored audience soon changes channels. Consequently, a three-foot-deep flood in Mississippi that will dry up in a few days may get greater coverage than a debate in Congress that may result in legislation that will affect the entire United States.

This is not to say that news programs do not present some excellent documentaries on important topics that lack spectacular film footage. For example, in 1982, all three networks produced reports on the campaign contributions and lobbying efforts of political action committees (PACs). There wasn't much action for the cameras,

(66)

but because PACs have such a strong impact on the American democratic system, the subject received substantial air time. Although some people would like to see PAC activities reported continually, if the networks had never brought the matter to nationwide attention, most people might never even have heard about them.

## TELEVISION AND
## THE ART OF PROTEST

Special interest groups, from pacifist demonstrators to Palestine Liberation Organization (PLO) guerrillas, have exploited television's penchant for news with action. A classic example occurred during the 1982 antinuclear arms-race rally in New York City. Protesters and police agreed beforehand that a few protesters would be allowed to block traffic by lying down in the street. After a few minutes, the protesters would submit to a passive and largely symbolic arrest. The purpose of the charade was not to irk motorists but rather to provide action for news cameras. Network news departments were informed of exactly what would happen so that they could be at the scene on time and so that forty million Americans would get the impression that the arrest of the protesters was the big news of the day and that the antinuclear movement was worthy of national attention.

This passive cooperation between protesters, police, and media is a recent refinement in the art of using the media to air grievances. At the 1968 Democratic Convention in Chicago there was no such cooperation. Antiwar protesters incited police brutality to which they then subjected themselves. The news cameras were quite willing to leave the monotony of the convention to go outside and catch a very convenient riot. The protesters chanted "The whole world is watching" as they confronted the police. The world did indeed watch, and the antiwar movement gained a lot of attention and considerable sympathy.

Yasir Arafat, leader of the PLO, has used the news media with great effectiveness to further the cause of his organization. With terrorist attacks such as the kidnapping and murder of Israeli athletes at the Munich Olympics in 1976, the PLO was not aiming for military conquest as much as international attention and recognition of the Palestinian people. Other organizations such as the Irish Republican Army (IRA) and the Red Brigades know that their acts of terrorism will never defeat their enemies, but with the help of television and other media, their bombs and complaints are heard around the world.

The Iranians who took over the U.S. embassy in Tehran in 1979 soon realized that they had captured more than people and property. They had the eyes and ears of the world. They also had a message for America. The American media were reluctantly willing to help them send that message in order to bring the American audience some information about the situation. Many say that NBC went too far, however, when they made a deal to air a statement by the hostage-takers in exchange for an interview with a hostage. Such use of the media is exactly what terrorists want, and the networks and other media have a general policy of reporting terrorism but not directly working with the terrorists.

THE LYING EYE

An age-old proverb advises: "Believe nothing you hear and only half of what you see." This certainly holds true in the age of television. Even the most honest and conscientious television report cannot show the whole picture. The camera has to focus on one thing at a time and the editors who assemble the various camera shots into a news report have to cut out parts and then put the rest into some sort of order. Although this is done without any intention of deceiving the audience, the resulting report is necessarily not the whole truth. The trouble is, because of the power of television, the audience tends to think they have seen exactly what happened.

The hostage crisis in Iran was an exellent example of television cameras showing only part of a situation. For 444 days, Americans saw angry mobs burning effigies of Uncle Sam and waving placards written in English. The impression that most Americans got was that the entire country of Iran was one big riot. In reality, however, most of the action was on just one street, in front of the embassy where the world's television cameras came to capture some action. When the cameras arrived, the crowds went wild. When the cameras left, the people settled down. And meanwhile, a good part of the Iranian population, wisely quiet, thought that the Ayatollah Khomeini was ruining their country. But what did Americans and the rest of the world see on television? They saw only what the cameras showed them—the mob at the embassy—and they assumed they were seeing all of Iran. The effect on the American public almost started a war.

The extraordinarily popular "60 Minutes" has often been accused of showing only half a story. Its audience share of over 50 percent puts it consistently among the top programs on the air, and its one thousand incoming letters per week testify that people do more than just watch. They become involved, they believe what they see, and they trust that "60 Minutes" is telling them the whole truth.

But many of the people and institutions that the show's reporters—Harry Reasoner, Morley Safer, Mike Wallace, and others—investigate feel that "60 Minutes" is only showing part of the truth, the part that the reporters choose to show. With clever and sometimes devious techniques, they say, "60 Minutes" is abusing the powers of television. By cutting out as much as 98 percent of an interview, for example, the investigators are not allowing the accused to explain their side of the story. Fifty million people see the "60 Minutes" side, yet the other side has no opportunity to defend itself or even explain that what the audience saw on television may have been out of context and contrived to look worse than it really was.

"60 Minutes" and other shows like it certainly are not trying to make the innocent look guilty, but Mike Wallace admits that he and his crew "have the power to convey any picture we want. . . . All we have to do is use different parts of the same interview."

What Wallace admits is exactly what newscaster Daniel Schorr has accused him of. In 1976 "60 Minutes" interviewed Schorr about a CIA report he had illegally publicized because he thought the American public should know about it. The unedited interview was seventy-five minutes long, but the version that went on the air was only thirteen minutes long. In the part aired, Schorr admitted what he had done; the parts cut out were his reasons for doing it—some very interesting reasons that revealed a man under pressure and in doubt as to the correct action to take. But "60 Minutes" did not choose to tell that part of his story. Schorr, not having a television show of his own or access to a skilled production crew and thirteen minutes of primetime on a network, had no way to explain his side of what happened. The problem is not limited to this incident or to "60 Minutes." Such programs are often a sort of trial that can sway the opinions of millions of Americans without allowing the accused, guilty or innocent, to defend themselves.

## TELEVISION, POLITICS, AND THE PRESIDENT

Television's wide and heterogeneous audience, combined with its ability to manipulate truth into half-truth or even outright untruth, make it an ideal tool for political persuasion and propaganda. Fortunately, the United States and other democracies have not allowed their governments to use television to promote their own power, to suppress contrary ideas, or to unfairly control national opinion. But television and government are by no means strangers to each other in America.

The president of the United States has unparalleled access to network television. Although he cannot demand time, his formal requests are almost always requested. One of the very few exceptions occurred when President Carter wanted to wish all Americans a happy new year live from the Shah's palace in Tehran. All three networks refused on the grounds that the subject was not of national importance.

The ability to appear on prime-time television at will gives the president and his party an excellent opportunity to explain their points of view, which gives them a tremendous political advantage. Polls indicate that a president's popularity always rises just after a televised speech or news conference. To try to balance this advantage, when the president speaks on a controversial topic the networks usually offer time for rebuttals from the opposing party. That these rebuttals are less effective than the words of the president is due to the difference in the importance of the speakers, not to the failure of the networks.

President Reagan said that much of his success in getting his economic policies through Congress was due to the prime-time coverage of his speeches. By carefully explaining his ideas and urging Americans to write to their representatives, he managed to put strong pressure on Congress. According to opinion polls, those who expressed opposing opinions immediately after his speeches were not nearly as persuasive.

## TELEVISION AND
## THE DEMOCRATIC PROCESS

Television has brought a new dimension to democracy. During the first years of American history, most voters never heard the speeches or saw the faces of the candidates running for office. Although it doesn't say much for the electoral process, it is true that physical appearance, mannerisms, and tone of voice influence voters as much as the opinions and qualifications of the candidates. It has been speculated that Abraham Lincoln, who was not a physically attractive man, would never have been elected if television had shown all Americans what he looked like. Richard Nixon suffered such a demise in the election of 1960. When he debated John F. Kennedy on television just before the election, Kennedy appeared cool, calm, intelligent, and handsome. Candidate Nixon had poor makeup and appeared nervous. People who saw the debate on television thought Kennedy won; those who heard it on the radio thought Nixon won. In the election, Kennedy became president by a slim margin, and it may have been Nixon's poor physical appearance on television that made the difference.

This does not mean that television is seriously impairing the rational decisions of voters. Quite to the contrary, television is bringing voters more information about candidates than was ever before possible. The candidates are always on camera and are easily caught if they make unwise remarks or contradictory promises along the campaign trail. Since it is so easy for Americans to hear the key points of several speeches and interviews, virtually all voters can walk into the voting booth with a reasonably good understanding of each candidate's position on the major issues.

A study conducted in 1969 found that 70 percent of American adults use television to learn about candidates and campaigns. Aware of this, campaign managers plan their campaigns accordingly. Flight schedules, major announcements, and events are timed to allow cameras to record the action and prepare it for the evening news. If cameras are expected, nothing will happen until they arrive. Statements are then kept short and simple enough to fit into thirty or forty second reports. Likewise, tough questions are best answered with statements too long and confusing to put on the air.

During the 1980 election, Ronald Reagan reserved twenty-two of the fifty-one seats on his campaign plane for reporters from the three networks. His press secretary went further to win network friendship by providing them with news releases and speech transcripts that were not available to other reporters. And whenever possible, a helicopter would ferry the candidate to an appointment, thus providing the action that attracts television cameras.

Television viewers, however, get most of their information about the candidates not from the news but from political advertisements. During the 1980 elections, Jimmy Carter and Ronald Reagan each allocated about 60 percent of their $29.4 million campaign budgets to television advertising. As in all elections since 1952, when televised political advertising began, the advertisements are planned and produced by advertising agencies that know how to make a product appealing to great numbers of people. In the case of political advertising, the product for sale is a political candidate.

*Advertising Age* magazine said that the close race between Gerald Ford and Jimmy Carter in 1976 was won by the candidate with the best advertising. Jimmy Carter made the wise choice to use television more than other media. This let America meet the candidate who had been virtually unknown a few months earlier, and let them fall in love with his honest face and charming smile. To stretch his television funds further, Carter made special commercials aimed at specific audiences. Rather than buy expensive prime-time spots that would hit a larger number of people, he would aim, for example, an advertisement at women voters and schedule it for afternoon soap operas. On a program with a large black audience, the advertisement would not say "Vote for Carter," which he knew they would do anyway, but rather "Be sure to vote," which blacks have tended not to do.

All of this seems to indicate that the candidate who wins is the one who can best exploit the media, especially television, with well-planned events and well-designed advertisements. To a certain extent this is true, but the media manipulation contest also serves as a test for the candidate most capable of organizing things and persuading people to follow the leader.

There is concern that the candidate that can afford to buy the most air time is more likely to win. Because air time is so expensive and so important, the cost of campaigns has risen so high that serious contenders for office must have a tremendous amount of money. Those without the financial support of big business and a major political party stand little chance of winning, regardless of their qualifications.

Given money, however, candidates can use television as a tool to bring themselves to everyone's attention. An unknown with a small following and basic qualifications can make his or her face known throughout the country. Since almost everyone watches television, even those with no interest in politics cannot help but know who the candidates are and their basic though often shifting stances on the issues. To the extent that the audience is aware how the candidates use television, they can make more intelligent choices in the voting booth.

In the end, it is impossible to say whether television helps or hurts democracy. But it undeniably changes certain factors in the democratic process. And as television becomes an increasingly prevalent factor in the lives of Americans, it will have increasingly powerful effects on America.

# 8
# TELEVISION
# TOMORROW

The explosive growth of electronic technology promises an ever-increasing importance for television. Well over a hundred channels and broadcast sources are going to deliver an extraordinary variety of programs and information to every television set in America. Many new advances, such as communications satellites, cable systems, and low-power VHF stations are already in operation. In the near future, computers will enhance existent systems to a point where television is not primarily an entertainment medium but rather a cornerstone of American society.

## CABLE TELEVISION

Cable television has been in existence since the earliest days of television. Only recently, however, have great numbers of television sets been linked to cable systems. These systems transmit television signals by wire rather than over the air. In 1982 about 30 percent of American homes were connected to a local cable system. By 1990, over half will be.

Cable offers several advantages over VHF and UHF television. Since the signals are not sent over the air, the video image is not distorted by distance or atmospheric conditions. More important is the number of channels that cable can carry. The first cable systems carried about thirty channels, but some have already expanded to eighty. Eventually that number will exceed one hundred. This allows for a much greater variety of programming. A few of the channels carry local and distant VHF or UHF transmissions. Others carry special programming such as uninterrupted movies from the Home Box Office (HBO) syndicate or children's programs from the Nickelodeon syndicate. Other channels may be reserved for education and local public affairs. Many communities require their area's cable company to provide a public-access channel. These channels are reserved for individuals and special interest groups that want an opportunity to speak to the entire community.

## COMMUNICATIONS SATELLITES

In the past decade, communications satellites have made it possible to beam broadcasts from a single source to an unlimited number of local broadcast stations and home television sets. In 1980 there were eighty such satellites in orbit and by 1985 there will be fifty more. These satellites, 22,300 miles above the earth, are in geosynchronous orbit, traveling in the same direction as the earth's rotation and at a speed that keeps them at the same point above the earth's surface. A television signal sent to one of these satellites bounces back to cover an area that can include half the globe, giving them a tremendous advantage over normal television transmissions, which reach only to the horizon.

Most of the receivers of these satellite signals are unaffiliated VHF and UHF stations and cable television stations. The Independent Network News, produced by WPIX in New York City, is beamed to about forty other stations. The Spanish International network sends programs from Spain and Latin America to U.S. cities with large Hispanic communities. Home Box Office and Nickelodeon transmit special programs to local cable stations which then send the programs to subscribers who are connected to the cable system. Depending on the type of programming, these receiving stations either pay for programs without commercials or receive programs with commercials in an agreement much like those between the networks and their affiliates.

In 1982 the FCC allowed private homes and apartment complexes to receive satellite signals with their own earth-receiving antennae, which are now available for as little as $300. Many of the programs that these antennae can receive come with commercials, so the broadcasters are glad to have the audience tune in. But for commercial-free programs, such as Home Box Office movies, this is a problem. The right to receive these programs is sold to local broadcasters who then, in effect, sell the programs to their audience by putting in commercials or charging a fee for the use of the cable channel that carries the program to the audience. To prevent unauthorized reception of the programs, the television signals are electronically scrambled at the original broadcast source. The local stations that receive the signals have special devices that unscramble the signals, making them normal again. This is not a perfect solution, however, because some people have bought and are illegally using these devices to "steal" signals from the satellites. But legally or otherwise, home earth-receiving stations are making it possible for any given television set to receive dozens of new television channels.

## LOW-POWER VHF STATIONS

Even more channels are becoming available since a 1982 FCC decision that allows the building of low-power VHF stations. These stations will broadcast only within a twenty-mile radius. Since their power is limited, they can use locally vacant VHF channels without interfering with the broadcasts of nearby cities. This will allow any local area to have programs on all twelve VHF channels. Since this is the first time in many years that new stations can be built in major cities, the FCC is already swamped with requests for licenses from entrepreneurs, universities, school boards, and religious, ethnic, and other special interest groups.

## INTERACTIVE CABLE

A two-way cable system allows not only signals from the broadcaster to the individual television set, but from the owner of the set to other points in the cable system. Such systems are still in the experimental stage, but since 1977 a system called Qube has been operating in Columbus, Ohio.

Qube combines two of the most important technological advances of the twentieth century—the television and the computer. An event most indicative of what QUBE can do was a specially arranged football game between Columbus and another city. And it was quite literally that—the city of Columbus itself was playing. By punching numbers on their home controls, the people of Columbus voted on the best plays for their team. A computer counted the votes and relayed them to the Columbus quarterback, who was obliged to follow his "coach's" advice. The Columbus team lost, but a point was proven. A large part of the city's people had interacted through their television sets.

The potential of two-way television goes far beyond fun and games. From a political aspect, thousands of citizens can attend a town meeting by video and express their opinions by pushing buttons. If one or more channels were devoted to local, state, and national political matters, government would be under constant scrutiny and voters would have an instant means of "speaking" to their elected officials.

Two-way television could also become a video shopping center of products that viewers can order with armchair ease. They could even pay for the products by using the system to transfer money from their bank accounts to the store.

Two-way television could also become an extended education system. Children and adults could not only watch lectures on television, but they could also use their televisions to ask and answer questions. Video texts could be summoned to the screen from a computer memory. Nothing would prevent exceptionally bright high school students from taking college courses; adults could review basic courses they have forgotten since high school. It is even possible that schools themselves might become obsolete.

## THE COMPUTER CONNECTION

The marriage of television and the computer may soon make television the ultimate library. The memory of a powerful central computer—or several computers—may one day hold more television programs than a library holds books. The technology already exists for a computer to print words on a video screen. A system called videotex, in which all the televisions in a two-way cable system are connected to a computerized storehouse of information, is only a few years away. Subscribers to a videotex system will be able to have anything from French recipes to London subway maps displayed on their television screens.

Videotex may one day be rendered obsolete by computers with banks of video disks. Video disks, which hold recorded video programs much as phonograph records hold recorded music, are already on the market. As future electronics allows the miniaturization of these disks, a computerized "juke box" of tens of thousands of disks would give home televisions access to an enormous body of information. A television set with a few hundred cable and satellite channels might be able to connect with the computers of libraries, universities, corporations, and other institutions all over the world.

The possibilities of such a system are literally limitless. A television-computer system in an airport might have lists of restaurants and hotels, complete with prices, menus, and even a walking tour through the facilities. At home, a desire to commune with nature could be satisfied by requesting a disk that shows a hike through Yosemite during which the viewer could control the trip by making decisions at forks in the trail. People who read could request a book, page by page, from a library computer that would remember where the reader left off the day before. A hospital computer could show doctors anything from disease symptoms to surgical techniques.

*Science Digest* magazine has been looking even further into the future. One tantalizing possibility it envisioned was three-dimensional video wallpaper. If linked into a national cable or satellite network, the system would let people play video games with distant, unknown adversaries. The thrill of participating in a national championship of 3-D galactic battles would be awfully hard to ignore.

This book must end with many of the same questions that introduced it. Looking toward the future, the effects of television, good and bad, on adults, children, society, and politics are bound to intensify. Between the ever-expanding choices of entertainment and vast new fields of video information, people will be spending more time than ever in the company of their television sets.

Many of the negative aspects of today's television are caused by its dearth of choice. Educational, cultural, and documentary programs are scarce, children have little to choose from, and televised information as varied and voluminous as that of a library is simply not available. To many Americans, television is a dreary series of quiz shows, soap operas, police dramas, and half-witted sitcoms. "There's nothing on" often means there is no choice but the same old sex, violence, commercials, and general idiocy.

With over a hundred channels to choose from, however, Americans may find television worth watching all the time. At any given moment, twenty-four hours a day, there will be something of interest or importance on at least one channel. While television will always carry plenty of light entertainment, it may also become an important source—perhaps the principle source—of culture, education, and information. Anyone without a television would be handicapped, living with one eye closed to the world.

The day may come when carrying a television around will be as natural and important as having a wristwatch. In fact, in 1982, a Japanese company introduced a wrist-television. It only received one channel, but it may be an indication of things to come. As one American radio announcer who reported the news of the invention wryly added, "How long will it be until they put video screens inside our contact lenses?"

That might be going too far. But then again, it might let us see farther than we ever have before.

# FOR FURTHER READING

Two easily read textbooks—Donald R. Pember's *Mass Media in America* (Chicago: Science Research Associates, Inc., 1974) and Peter M. Sandman's *Media: An Introductory Analysis of American Mass Communications* (Englewood Cliffs, NJ: Prentice-Hall, 1982) have a lot of information on television and other media.

Marshall McLuhan's famous *Understanding Media: The Extensions of Man* (New York: McGraw-Hill, 1966) is hard to understand but a simpler version comes in his illustrated *The Medium Is the Massage* (New York: Bantam, 1967).

For some scathing views of the television industry, read Harry Skornia's *Television and Society* (New York: McGraw-Hill, 1965), Ben Stein's *The View From Sunset Boulevard* (New York: Doubleday, 1980), and Les Brown's *Television—The Business Behind the Box* (New York: Harcourt Brace Jovanovich, 1971).

Marie Winn's *The Plug-In Drug* (New York: Viking, 1977), and Gerald Lesser's *Children and Television: Lessons from Sesame Street* (New York: Random House, 1974) both deal with the effects of television on children.

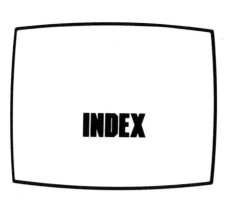

# INDEX

FCC (Federal Communications Commission), 9–10, 20, 32, 78, 79; children's television and, 34, 58–59; powers defined, 23–25
Future of television, 76–83

Galbraith, John Kenneth, 35
Government control, 6, 13–14, 23–28, 59; see also FCC

HBO (Home Box Office), 77–78

Independent stations, 11, 78
Influence summarized, 2–7
Iranian hostage crisis, 68–69

Kennedy, John F., 72

McLuhan, Marshall, 37–40, 84
"Mister Rogers' Neighborhood," 3, 56, 57
Monopolies, 24, 27

National Association of Broadcasters (NAB), 26–28
National Institute of Mental Health, 48, 62
NBC (National Broadcasting Corporation), 9, 47, 58, 68
Network system, 9–12
News, 3, 4, 40, 64–69; editing, 3, 68–71
Nielsen Company, A.C., 17–20
Nickelodeon, 77–78
Nixon, Richard, 13–14, 72–73
Normality, perceptions of, 41–44; see also Reality

Paranoia, social, 6, 48
Passivity, 54, 57
PBS (Public Broadcasting System), 12–15, 54–60
Plug-In Drug (Winn), 54, 85
Political action committees (PACs), 66–67

Political coverage, 71–75
Presidential access to television, 71–72
Protest coverage, 67–68
Public-interest requirement, 24–25, 77
Public television, 12–15, 54–60

Qube, 79–80

Ratings, 16–20, 56, 58
Reagan, Ronald, 59, 72–74
Reality misrepresented, 2, 3, 41–44, 45–47, 68–71

Satellites, communications, 77–79
Schorr, Daniel, 70
Self-regulation, industry, 26–28
"Sesame Street," 14, 55–57
Sex, 22, 24, 50–52
Singer, Jerome, 61–62
"60 Minutes," 69–71
Soap operas, 44, 50, 51
Socialization, 40–42; see also Behavior
Special interest groups, 6, 20–21, 22–23
Syndicates, program, 11

Television Code, 27–28
Terrorism, 66, 68
Two-way cable, 79–80

UHF, 10, 77, 78
Understanding Media: The Extensions of Man (McLuhan), 38–40, 84

VHF, 9–10, 77, 78; low-power, 79
Videotex, 81
Violence, 22, 45–49, 53, 58

Women, portrayal of, 42